ACCOUNTANCY

PART-2

:: Author ::

ROBIN N. VORA

(M.COM., B.ED., SLET)
GUJARAT UNIVERSITY RANKER

PUBLISHED BY

The New Era International Publishing House
HQ. At & Po. Chaveli., Ta- Chansma,
Dist- Patan, North Gujarat, India, Asia.

First Publication: 5th FEBRUARY, 2015

Copyright: Author
(c) ROBIN N. VORA

ISBN:- 978-15-08472-69-8

Price: Rs.750/- INDIA
    $ 15 OUTSIDE INDIA

PUBLISHED BY

The New Era International Publishing House
HQ. At & Po. Chaveli., Ta- Chansma,
Dist- Patan, North Gujarat, India, Asia.

Dedicated
to
my
Parents

INDEX

CHAPTER – 1
("Ledger Posting")

☐ THEORY SECTION ☐

In the Journal, each transaction is dealt with separately. Therefore, it is not possible to know at a glance, the net result of many transactions.So, in order to ascertain the net effect of all the transactions relating to a particular account are collected at one place in the Ledger.

A Ledger is a book which contains all the accounts Whether personal, real or nominal, which are first entered in journal or special purpose subsidiary books.

According to **L.C. Cropper**, 'the book which contains a Classified and permanent record of all the transactions of a business is called the Ledger'.

The ledger that is normally used in a majority of business Concern is a bound note book. This can be preserved for a long time. Its pages are consequently numbered. Each account in the ledger is opened preferably on a separate page. If one page is completed, the account will be continued in the next or some other page. But in bigger concerns, it is not practical to keep the ledger as a bound note book, Loose-lea ledger now takes the place of a bound note book. In a loose-leaf ledger,appropriate ruled sheets of thick paper are introduced and fixed up with the help of a binder. Whenever necessary additional pages may be inserted, completed accounts can be removed and the accounts may be arranged and rearranged in the desired order. Therefore, this type of ledger is known as **Loose-leaf Ledger**.

Utility

Ledger is a principal or main book which contains all the Accounts in which the transactions recorded in the books of Original entry are transferred. Ledger is also called the **'Book of Final Entry'** or **'Book of Secondary Entry'**, because the transactions are finally incorporated in the Ledger.

The following are the advantages of ledger.

i. Complete information at a glance:
All the transactions pertaining to an account are collected at one place in the ledger. By looking at the balance of that account, one can understand the collective effect of all such transactions at a glance.

ii. Arithmetical Accuracy
With the help of ledger balances, Trial balance can be prepared to know the arithmetical accuracy of accounts.

iii. Result of Business Operations
It facilitates the preparation of final accounts for ascertaining the operating result and the financial position of the business concern.

iv. Accounting information

The data supplied by various ledger accounts are

summarised, analysed and interpreted for obtaining various accounting information.

Format

Name of Account

Dr   *Cr*

Date	Particulars	J.F	Rs.	Date	Particulars	J.F	Rs.
Year Month Date	To (Name of Credit Account in Journal)			Year Month Date	By (Name of Debit account in Journal)		

Explanation:

i. *Each ledger account is divided into two parts. The left hand side is known as the debit side and the right hand side is known as the credit side. The words 'Dr.' and 'Cr.' are used to denote Debit and Credit.*

ii. *The name of the account is mentioned in the top (middle) of the account.*

iii. *The date of the transaction is recorded in the date column.*

iv. *The word 'To' is used before the accounts which appear on the debit side of an account in the particulars column. Similarly, the word 'By' is used before the accounts which appear on the credit side of an account in the particulars column.*

v. *The name of the other account which is affected by the transaction is written either in the debit side or credit side in the particulars column.*

vi. *The page number of the Journal or Subsidiary Book from where that particular entry is transferred, is entered in the Journal Folio (J.F) column.*

vii. *The amount pertaining to this account is entered in the amount column.*

Posting :

The process of transferring the entries recorded in the journal or subsidiary books to the respective accounts opened in the ledger is called Posting. In otherwords, posting means grouping of all the transactions relating to a particular account at one place. It is necessary to post all the journal entries into various accounts in the ledger because posting helps us to know the net effect of various transactions during a given period on a particular account.

Procedure of posting :

The procedure of posting is given as follows:

I. **Procedure of posting for an Account which has been debited in the journal entry.**

Step 1 *Locate in the ledger, the account to be debited and enter the date of the transaction in the date column on the debit side.*

Step 2 *Record the name of the account credited in the Journal in the particulars column on the debit side as "To..... (name of the account credited)".*

Step 3 *Record the page number of the Journal in the J.F column on the debit side and in the Journal, write the page number of the ledger on which a particular account appears in the L.F. column.*

Step 4   *Enter the relevant amount in the amount column on the debit side.*

II. **Procedure of posting for an Account which has been credited in the journal entry.**

Step 1   *Locate in the ledger the account to be credited and enter the date of the transaction in the date column on the credit side.*

Step 2   *Record the name of the account debited in the Journal in the particulars column on the credit side as "By...... (name of the account debited)"*

Step 3   *Record the page number of the Journal in the J.F column on the credit side and in the Journal, write the page number of the ledger on which a particular account appears in the L.F. column.*

Step 4   *Enter the relevant amount in the amount column on the credit side.*

Balancing an Account

Balance is the difference between the total debits and the total credits of an account. When posting is done, many accounts may have entries on their debit side as well as credit side. The net result of such debits and credits in an account is the balance. Balancing means the writing of the difference between the amount columns of the two sides in the lighter (smaller total) side, so that the grand totals of the two sides become equal.

Significance of balancing:

There are three possibilities while balancing an account during a given period. It may be a debit balance or a credit balance or a nil balance depending upon the debit total and the credit total.

i. **Debit Balance :** *The excess of debit total over the credit total is called the* **debit balance**. *When there is only debit entries in an account, the amount itself is the balance of that account, i.e., the debit balance. It is first recorded on the credit side, above the total. Then it is entered on the debit side, below the total, as the first item for the next period.*

ii. **Credit Balance :** *The excess of credit total over the debit total is called the* **credit balance**. *When there is only credit entries in an account, the amount itself is the balance of that account i.e., the credit balance. It is first written in the debit side, as the last item, above the total. Then it is recorded on the credit side, below the total, as the first item for the next period.*

Balancing of different accounts

Balancing is done periodically, i.e., weekly, monthly, quarterly, half-yearly or yearly, depending on the requirements of the business.

i.Personal Accounts : *These accounts are generally balanced regularly to know the amounts due to the persons* (**creditors**) *ordue from the persons* (**debtors**).

ii.Real Accounts : *These accounts are generally balanced at the end of the financial year, when final accounts are being prepared.However, cash account is frequently balanced to know the* **cash on hand.***A debit balance in an asset account indicated the* **value of the asset** *owned by the business. Assets accounts always show debit balances.*

iii. Nominal Accounts : *These accounts are in fact, not to be balanced as they are to be closed by transfer to final accounts. A debit balance in a nominal account indicates that it is* **an expense or loss.** *A credit balance in a nominal account indicates that it is* **an income or gain.***
All such balances in personal and real accounts are shown in the Balance Sheet and the balances in nominal accounts are taken to the Profit and Loss Account.*

Procedure for Balancing :

While balancing an account, the following steps are involved:

Step 1

Total the amount column of the debit side and the credit side separately and then ascertain the difference of both the columns.

Step 2

If the debit side total exceeds the credit side total, put such difference on the amount column of the credit side, write the date on which balancing is being done in the date column and the words **"By Balance c/d"** *(c/d means carried down) in the particulars column.*

*If the credit side total exceeds the debit side total, put such difference on the amount column of the debit side, write the date on which balancing is being done in the date column and the words "**To Balance c/d**" in the particulars column.*

Step 3

Total again both the amount columns, put the total on both the sides and draw a line above and a line below the totals.

Step 4

*Enter the date of the beginning of the next period in the date column and bring down the debit balance on the debit side along with the words "**To Balance b/d**" (b/d means brought down) in the particulars column and the credit balance on the credit side along with the words "**By balance b/d**" in the particulars column.*

Note: *In the place of **c/d** and **b/d**, the words **c/f** or **c/o** (carried forward or carried over) and **b/f** or **b/o** (brought forward or brought over) may also be used. When the balance is carried down **in the same page**, the words c/d and b/d are used, while balance is carried over **to the next page**, the term c/o and b/o are used. When balance is carried forward **to some other page** either in same book or some other book, the abbreviations c/f (carried forward) and b/f (brought forward) are used.*

Distinction between Journal and Ledger :

Basis of Distinction	Journal	Ledger
1. Book	It is the book of prime entry.	It is the main book of account.
2. Stage	Recording of entries in these books is the first	Recording of entries in the ledger is the
3. Process	The process of recording entries in these books is called "Journalising".	The process of recording entries in the ledger is called
4. Transactions	Transactions relating to a person or property or expense are spread over.	Transactions relating to a particular account are found together on
5. Net effect	The final position of a particular account can not be found.	The final position of a particular account can be ascertained just at
6. Next Stage	Entries are transferred to the ledger.	From the Ledger, first the Trial Balance is drawn and then final accounts
7. Tax authorities	Do not rely upon these Books	Rely on the ledger for assessment purpose.

□ PRACTICAL SECTION □

1. Journalise the following transactions in the books of Amar and post them in the Ledger:-

2014

March1	Bought goods for cash **Rs.** 25,000
2	Sold goods for cash **Rs.** 50,000
3	Bought goods for credit from Gopi **Rs.** 29,000
5	Sold goods on credit to Robert **Rs.** 8,000
7	Received from Robert **Rs.** 8,000
9	Paid to Gopi **Rs.** 10,000
20	Bought furniture for cash **Rs.** 7,000

2. Journalise the following transactions of Mr.Ravi and post them in the ledger and balance the same.

2011

June 1	Ravi invested **Rs.** 6,00,000 cash in the business
3	Paid into Bank **Rs.** 80,000
5	Purchased building for **Rs.** 2,00,000
7	Purchased goods for **Rs.** 70,000
10	Sold goods for **Rs.** 60,000
15	With drew cash from bank **Rs.** 40,000
25	Paid electric charges **Rs.** 3,000
30	Paid Salary **Rs.** 15,000

3.Record the following transactions in the Journal of Mr.Radhakrishnan and post them in the ledger and balance the same.

2015

Jan. 1 Radhakrishnan commenced businesswith cash,
     Rs. 18,00,000.

  3   Paid into Bank **Rs.** 5,50,000

  5   Bought goods for **Rs.** 3,80,000

  7   Paid travelling charges **Rs.** 50,000

  10 Sold goods for **Rs.** 2,50,000

  15 Sold goods to Balan **Rs.** 2,40,000

  20 Purchased goods from Narayanan **Rs.** 2,10,000

  25 Withdrew cash **Rs.** 80,000

4. Enter the following transactions in journal and post them in the ledger of Mr.Govindarajan and balance them.

2013,

  Aug 1 Govindarajan commenced his business with the following assets and liabilities.

       Plant and Machinery **Rs.** 2,00,000.

       Stock **Rs.** 99,000.

       Furniture **Rs.** 70,000.

       Cash **Rs.** 30,000.

       Sundry creditors **Rs.** 1,40,000.

  2   Sold goods to Sundar **Rs.** 1,80,000.

  3   Bought goods from Natarajan **Rs.** 55,000.

  4   Sundar paid cash **Rs.** 1,15,000.

  6   Returned damaged goods to Natarajan **Rs.** 2,000.

  10 Paid to Natarajan **Rs.** 28,000.

  31 Paid rent **Rs.** 5,000.

       Paid salaries **Rs.** 9,000.

5. *Journalise the following transactions in the Journal of Mr.Shanmugam, post them in the ledger and balance them.*

2014,

Aug.	*1*	*Started business with* **Rs.** *4,00,000*
	3	*Goods purchased* **Rs.** *70,000*
	5	*Goods sold* **Rs.** *58,000*
	10	*Goods purchased from Rangasamy* **Rs.** *2,10,000*
	16	*Goods returned to Rangasamy* **Rs.** *5,000*
	23	*Drew from bank* **Rs.** *30,000*
	26	*Furniture purchased* **Rs.** *11,000*
	27	*Settled Rangasamy's account*
	31	*Salaries paid,* **Rs.** *22,000*

……..xxxxxxxxx……

CHAPTER – 2
("Trial Balance")

□ THEORY SECTION □

Trial balance is a statement which shows debit balances and Credit balances of all accounts in the ledger. Since, every debit should have a corresponding credit as per the rules of double entry system, the total of the debit balances and credit balances should tally (agree). In case, there is a difference, one has to check the correctness of the balances brought forward from the respective accounts. Trial balance can be prepared in any date provided accounts are balanced.

Definition :
"Trial balance is a statement, prepared with the debit and Credit balances of ledger accounts to test the arithmetical accuracy of the books" – **J.R. Batliboi**.

Objectives :

The objectives of preparing a trial balance are:
  i.   To check the arithmetical accuracy of the ledger accounts.
  ii. To locate the errors.
  iii. To facilitate the preparation of final accounts.

Advantages

The advantages of the trial balance are

i. It helps to ascertain the arithmetical accuracy of the book-keeping work done during the period.

ii. It supplies in one place ready reference of all the balances of the ledger accounts.

iii. If any error is found out by preparing a trial balance, the same can be rectified before preparing final accounts

iv. It is the basis on which final accounts are prepared.

Methods :

A trial balance can be prepared in the following methods.

i. **The Total Method :** According to this method, the total amount of the debit side of the ledger accounts and the total amount of the credit side of the ledger accounts are recorded.

ii. **The Balance Method :** In this method, only the balances of an account either debit or credit, as the case may be, are recorded against their respective accounts.

The balance method is more widely used, as it supplies ready figures for preparing the final accounts.

Format :

Name of account	L.F.	Debit Rs.	Credit Rs.

Points to be noted :

i.   Date on which trial balance is prepared should be mentioned at the top.

ii.   Name of Account column contains the list of all ledger accounts.

iii. Ledger folio of the respective account is entered in the next column.

iv.   In the debit column, debit balance of the respective account is entered.

v.   Credit balance of the respective account is written in the credit column.

vi.   The last two columns are totalled at the end.

Limitations :

Though the trial balance helps to ensure the arithmetical Accuracy of the books of accounts, it is possible only when the accountant has not committed any error. As all the errors made are not disclosed by the trial balance, it would not be regarded as a conclusive proof of correctness of the books of accounts maintained.

☐ PRACTICAL SECTION ☐

1. **The following balances have been taken from the books of Shri Jheel as on 31-12-2000 prepare a trial balance as a statement from the same :**

Name of the Account	Balance Rs.	Name of the Account	Balance Rs.
Capital	42,080	Commission Received	300
Drawings	2,000	Bank Commission	70
Debtors	8,750	Lighting exp	1,240
Creditors	7,120	Wages	300
Cash	17,610	Salary	1,000
Furniture	5,000	Goods destroyed by fire	3,000
Bank	7,980	Goods withdrawn for personal use	1,000
6.5 % Government Loan	5,000	Loan borrowed from Parvati	5,000
Opening Stock	15,000	Discount Allowed	1,000
Purchase	14,650	Discount received	300
Sales	21,200	Carriage	200
Purchase Returns	1,850	Loss by fire	800
Sales Return	1,250		

2. **From the following balance taken from the books of Shri Ashish as on 31-3-2008 prepare a trial balance in the form of an account.**

Name of the Account	Balance Rs.	Name of the Account	Balance Rs.
Capital	14,800	Stationary	400
Purchase	27,600	Conveyance exp	600
Customers	26,400	Drawings	3,600

Cartage	2,400	Royalty (Cr)	2,600
Taxes	1,700	Goods Return-Debit	1,400
Cash balance	3,100	Suppliers	8,400
Rent	1,200	Wages	7,000
Shyam Brothers (Dr)	800	Miscellaneous exp	3,400
Contribution to Gujarat Gaurav Day	2,000	Bills payable	16,000
Sales	72,000	Vehicles	6,000
Goods Return- Credit	600	Discount received	1,000
Stock of goods			
Salary	16,800	Sample exp	200
Bills Receivable	8,400	Goodwill	2,000
	2,000		

……..xxxxxxxx……

CHAPTER – 3
("Bad Debts And Provision For Doubtful Debts")

□ THEORY SECTION □

❖ *Types of Receivables :*

    a) Good debts : *Out of the total amount of total debtors or receivables the amount which is going to be recovered certainly and there is no doubt regarding its recovery, is known as good debts.*

    b) Bad debts : *The amount for which it is clear that it is not going to be recovered is known as bad debts.*

    c) Doubtful debts : *Those receivables for which there is no guarantee regarding its recovery and its recovery is doubtful, is known as doubtful debts.*

✗ *Discount Reserve (Debit) on Debtors (DRD) :*

    According to traditions and customs of the business, customers are given the benefit of cash discount as an incentive to pay their dues earlier. As this discount is an expense for a trader, in the books of accounts cash discount given to customers, is debited as an expense. This discount is known as debit discount.

    On the basis of past years' experiences and business custom a trader calculates a probable amount of discount to be given to such debtors in next year and for it, a reserve is created from the profit and loss a/c. It is known as a discount reserve on debtors.

☆ *Accounting Entries for Bad debts and Bad debts reserve (Provision for Doubtful Debts) :*

1) *Cash A/c   Dr.*

   *To Bad debt return A/c (**Amount of Bad debt recovered**)*

2) *Bad debt A/c   Dr.*

   *To Debtors A/c (**New bad debt which is given in Adjustment or Additional information**)*

3) *Bad debts reserve A/c   Dr.*

   *To Bad debt A/c   (**Total bad debt = Old bad debt + New bad debt**)*

4) *Profit & Loss A/c   Dr.*

   To Bad debts reserve A/c

(Amount of P & L A/c = Total bad debt + Closing balance of BDR {which is given in Adjustment } – Opening balance of BDR{which is given in Trial balance})

NOTE NO.1 : IF THE ABOVE AMOUNT COMES IN MINUS (-) THEN THE ABOVE JOURNAL (No. 4) JUST DO REVERSE)

5) *Discount Reserve on debtors A/c   Dr.*
*   To Discount A/c* **(Amount of discount allowed which is given in Trail balance** *)*

6) *Profit & Loss A/c   Dr.*
*   To Discount Reserve on debtors A/c*

(Amount of P & L A/c = Amount of discount allowed + Closing balance of DRD {which is given in Adjustment } – Opening balance of DRD {which is given in Trial balance})

NOTE NO.2 : IF ABOVE AMOUNT COMES IN MINUS (-) THEN THE ABOVE JOURNAL (No.6) JUST DO REVERSE)

☐ PRACTICAL SECTION ☐

1. From the following details of Rekhaben write necessary journal entries, discount a/c, reserve (debit) A/c, and bad debt reserve account and show the effects in final accounts. Extract to trial balance as on 31-3-2014

Particulars	L.f	Debit Balance Rs.	Credit Balance Rs.
Debtors		28,600	
Bad debts		700	
Discount		800	
Bad debts reserve (opening balance)			500
Discount reserve on debtors (opening balance)			300

Adjustments:

1) *Write off additional bad debts* **Rs. 1600.**

2) *Provide for doubtful debts @* **Rs. 10%** *on debtors and discount reserve on debtors @ 5%.*

2. From the following information of Abbas agency prepare year wise bad debts account and bad debt reserve A/c. Year of agency ends on 31st December, show necessary effects in final accounts :

Name of Account	2011 Rs.	2012 Rs.
Bad debts	1200	600
Debtors	58200	60300
Bad debts return	500	400
Provision for doubtful debts	10%	5%

Adjustments:

1) As bad debts **Rs. 200** and **Rs. 300** is to be written off at the end of the year **2011** and **2012** respectively.

2) Balance of bad debts reserve account was **Rs. 4900** as on **1-1-2011**.

3. **The following information is given, from the trial balance of Jay.**

Particulars	Year 2002-03 Rs.	Year 2003-04 Rs.
Bad debt	3400	2500
Debtors	52100	61000
Bad debt recovered	600	500
Percentage for bad debt reserve	10%	8%

Adjustment:

☆ **Rs. 2,100** And **Rs. 1,000** in first and in second year respectively are to written off as bad debt.

☆ On **1-4-02** there was a balance **(Credit)** of **Rs. 11,600** of bad debt reserve A/c.

From the above information prepare year wise bad debt account and bad debt reserve account, and also show the effect in the final account of first year.

4. **The following is the information in a trial balance of Ram Ltd as on 31-3-2014**

Name of the Account	Debt Balance Rs.	Credit Balance Rs.
Debtors	61100	
Bad Debtors	900	
Bad Debt returned		300
Bad debt reserve (1-4-13)		4100
Discount reserve on debtors (1-4-13)		3000
Discount allowed	400	

> ➤ **Additional information :**

☆ *In current year, out of the debtors Anjana has shown her incapability of paying* **Rs. 1,100.** *For this accounting effects are to be recorded in the books.*

☆ *Provide reserve on doubtful debts at* **6 %** *and discount reserve on debtors at* **2%** *on debtors balance. Prepare necessary accounts and journal entries. Show the effects of above in final accounts.*

CHAPTER – 4
("ANNUAL ACCOUNTS")

☐ FORMULAS ☐

1) Adjusted purchase = Opening stock + Net Purchase – Closing stock
2) Cost of goods sold = Opening stock of goods + Purchase + Purchase Expense – Closing stock of goods

☐ IMPORTANT POINTS ☐

❋ **In Final Accounts of a Partnership Firm Prepare :**

1. Trading Account

2. Profit and Loss Account

3. Balance Sheet

NOTE : For the business concerns like Tuition classes, Beauty Parlous, Commercial Institutions, Consultation concerns, Hospitals, Dispensaries etc. It is not necessary to prepare Trading Account.

❋ **Remember :**

Name of Account	Reason	Result
Trading Account	a) Debit side is higher than credit side b) Credit side is higher than debit side	Gross Loss Gross Profit
Profit & Loss Account	a) Debit side is higher than credit side b) Credit side is higher than debit side	Net Loss Net Profit

Specimen of Trading Account

Trading Account of ………for the Year Ended………

Particulars	Rs.	Particulars	Rs.
To Opening Stock	………		
Purchase ………		By Sales ………	
Less:Pur.Returns …..	……..	Less : Sales Ret. …..	……
Expenses relating to Purchase		**Goods going out other then sales**	
Wages		By goods Destroyed by fire	……
Carriage inward	………	By goods given as charity	……
Railway freight	………	By goods withdrawn for personal use	……
Octroi	………	Goods distributed as free samples	……
Customs duty	………	Closing stock	……
Lorry Freight	………	Sales of scrap	……
Dock Charges	………		
Clearing charges	………		
Demurrage	………		
Darmayo	………		
Kharajat expenses	………		
Warfage	………		
Mahajan lago	………		
Expenses relating to production			
Productive wages	………		
Royalty	……..		

Factory expenses (rent, taxes, power & fuel, coal, gas)	....		
Material consumed (oil & Grease)	....		
Depreciation of factory Building, plant & Machine)	....		
To Gross Profit (Trans. to P & L A/c)	....	*By Gross Loss (Trans. to P & L A/c)*	
	....		....

Specimen of Profit and Loss Account

Profit & Loss Account of ....for the Year Ended............

Particulars	Rs.	Particulars	Rs.
To Gross Loss (Transferred from Trading A/c)	....	*By Gross profit (Transferred from Trading A/c)*	....
Format of Stationery Exp.		*Incomes (Revenues)*	
Stationery Stock (Opening)		Rent received	....
+Stationery-printing expenses.........		Commission received	....
– Stationery Stock (Closing)	....	Brokerage received	....

Selling & Distribution Exp.		_Adat received_	....
Carriage outward	....	_Interest on investment_	....
Commission of salesman	....	_Interest on loan given_	....
Advertisement exp & Packing exp	....	_interest on drawings_	....
Delivery van exp	....	_bad debts returned_	....
Financial exp.		_profit on sale of assets_	....
Interest on capital	....	_Sale of scrap_	....
Interest on B.O.D or bank loan taken	....	_Misc. income etc._	....
Bank charges & bank commission	....	**_Format of Discount Received_**	
Other Exp. & losses	....	_Dis.Rece._	
Donation		_Add:DRC (Adj.)........._	
Dep. on assets	....	_Less:DRC (T/B) ...._	....
Salary and Rent	....		
Insurance Premium	....		
Taxes & Audit fees	....		
Postage Expenses & Electricity exp	....		
Contribution to provident fund	....		
Loss by fire	....		
Receivable Claim	....		
Format of Bad debt			
_B.D. (T/B)_			
Add:B.D. (Adj.)			
Add:BDR (Adj.).....			
Less :BDR (T/B)...	....		

Format of Discount Allowed			
Dis. Allow.			
Add: DRD (Adj.)...			
Less :DRD (T/B)....	....		
To Net Profit (Trans. to Capital A/c)	....	**By Net Loss** (Trans. to Capital A/c)	....
	....		....

Specimen of Balance Sheet

Balance Sheet of Shree.........as on........

Liabilities	Rs.	Assets	Rs.
Format of Capital		**Fixed Assets**	
Opening balance		*Goodwill*	......
+ Additional in Capital...		*Land*	......
+ Interest on Capital		*Building*	......
Net Profit		*Leasehold assets*	....
Less:		*Machinery*	......
		Furniture & Fittings	......
Drawings		*Patent, trademark, copy right*	......
Interest on drawings......			
Net Loss	......	*Live Stock*	......
Reserves		*Vehicles*	......
general reserve	......	**Investments**	
		Government Securities	......
Capital reserve	......		
Secured Loans		*Investment of*	......

		provident Fund	
Loan taken from bank	......	Investment of Share	......
Institutional Loan	......	**Current Assets**	
Unsecured Loans		Dead Stock	......
Fixed deposit	......	Closing stock	......
Loan taken from friends	......	Debtors(Customers or Dues)	......
Current Liabilities & provision			
B.O.D	......	Cash balance	......
		Bank balance	......
Bills payable	......	Stores & Spare parts, Loose tools	......
Creditors(Suppliers or Debt)	......	Income due but not received	......
Outstanding Exp	......	Loan Given	......
Incomes received in advance	......	Bills receivable	......
provision for Tax	......	Loan given to employee	......
provident Fund	......	Advance paid for purchases	......
		Expenses paid in advance	......
		Preliminary Expenses	......
		Discount on Share or Debenture	......
	......		......

⇒   _**Important Adjustments : (Give Two Effects)**_

Sr. No	Adjustment	Effects
1.	**Closing Stock**	a) Trading A/c credit side b) Balance sheet asset side as an asset
2.	**Outstanding expense**	a) Trading or profit & loss a/c debit side - addition to the exp b) Balance sheet liabilities side as a liability
3.	**Prepaid exp**	a)Trading or profit & loss a/c debit side - deduction from the exp b)Balance sheet asset side as an asset
4.	**Income due but not received**	a)P & L a/c credit side - addition to the respective income. b)Balance sheet asset side as an asset
5.	**Income received in advance**	a)P & L a/c credit side - deduction the respective income. b)Balance sheet asset side as liability.
6.	**Interest on capital**	a) Profit & loss a/c debit side b) Balance sheet liabilities side- In format of capital(+)
7.	**Interest on drawing**	a) Profit & loss a/c credit side b) Balance sheet liabilities side- In format of capital (-)
8.	**Depreciation on assets**	a) Profit & loss a/c debit side b) Balance sheet - asset side deducted from respective asset

9.	Bad debts (New)	a) Profit & loss a/c debit side - In format of Bad debts (+) b) Balance sheet - asset side deducted from debtors
10.	Provision for doubtful debts (B.D.R.) (New)	a) Profit & loss a/c debit side - In format of Bad debts (+) b) Balance sheet - asset side deducted from debtors
11.	Discount reserve on debtors (New)	a) Profit & loss a/c debit side - In format of Discount (+) b) Balance sheet - asset side deducted from debtors
12.	Unrecorded purchase	a) Trading account debit side addition to purchase b) Balance sheet liabilities side as an addition to the creditors
13.	Unrecorded sales	a) Trading a/c credit side addition to sales b) Balance sheet liabilities side as an addition to the debtors
14.	Goods with-drawn for personal use & the same is not recorded	a) Trading a/c credit side as goods withdrawn for personal use b) Balance sheet liabilities side as deduction from the capital
15.	Goods destroyed by fire	a) Trading a/c credit side as goods given destroyed by fire b) P & L a/c debit side as loss due to fire
16.	Goods destroyed by	a) Trading a/c credit side as goods destroyed by fire

	fire & insurance company accepts a partial claim	b) Balance sheet asset side, insurance company as debtors & in P & L a/c loss due to fire as expense
17.	Stationery stock	a)P & L a/c debit side as deduction from Stationary expenses b)Balance sheet asset side as stationery stock
18.	Write off proportionate part of lease hold property	a)P & L a/c debit side b)Balance sheet asset side as deduction from the asset

❖ **Other Important Hidden Adjustments which are Given in Trial Balance : (Give Only One Effect)**

No	Adjustment	Effect
1.	Closing Stock	Balance sheet asset side as an asset
2.	Depreciation on assets	Profit & loss a/c debit side
3.	Closing Stock of Stationery	Balance sheet asset side as stationery stock
4.	Outstanding expense	Balance sheet liabilities side as a liability
5.	Income due but not received	Balance sheet asset side as an asset
6.	Income received in advance	Balance sheet liabilities side as a liability
7.	Prepaid exp	Balance sheet asset side as an asset
8.	Depreciation Fund	Balance sheet - asset side deducted from respective asset
9.	Provident Fund	Balance sheet liabilities side as a liability
10.	Investment of PF	Balance sheet asset side as an asset
11.	Apprentice Premium received in Adv.	Balance sheet liabilities side as a liability

NOTE :

- ➤ *BDR : Bad debt reserve*
- ➤ *DRD: Discount reserve on debtors*
- ➤ *DRC: Discount reserve on creditors*
- ➤ *B.O.D : Bank overdraft*
- ➤ *Adj.: Adjustment*
- ➤ *T/B: Trial balance*

PRACTICAL SECTION

1. Trial Balance of Prachi after preparing the Trading account is as follows :

Trial Balance of Prachi as on 31-3-2011

Name of the Account	L. F.	Debit Balance	Credit Balance
Trading Account			1,23,600
Capital And Drawings		32,000	2,91,600
Customers' and suppliers		1,50,000	1,02,000
Machinery		1,20,000	
Discount		24,000	1,600
Closing stock		36,000	
Investment in **12 %** debentures' and Interest On investment		80,000	1,600
Advertising a/c		24,000	
Carriage outward		3,360	
Bad debt and provision of bad Debts		1,600	2,760
Salary		24,000	

Taxes and Insurance	1,800	
Furniture	48,000	
Sale of Furniture (1-4-2010)		4,000
Cash Balance	4,000	
	5,27,160	5,27,160

- **Prepare final accounts considering the following particulars :**
  - ❖ *Goods withdrawn for household use of **Rs. 9,600** is not recorded.*
  - ❖ *Goods of **Rs. 16,000** are destroyed by fire in March, for which the insurance Company has accepted a claim of **Rs. 12800**.*
  - ❖ *Credit purchase of **Rs. 12,000** is to be recorded.*
  - ❖ ***12%** debentures were purchased on **1-10-2010**.*
  - ❖ *Expenses incurred for advertisement campaign at the beginning of the year transferred to advertisement suspense a/c. This expense is to be written off in **5** year.*
  - ❖ *The book value of furniture sold is **Rs. 6,000***
  - ❖ *Write off **Rs. 2,000** from debtors and provide **5 %** for bad debt reserve.*
  - ❖ *Calculate depreciation at **5 %** on furniture and **10 %** on machinery.*
  - ❖ *Brokerage of **Rs. 2,280** is yet to be received.*

2. **From the following Trial Balance of Mahesh prepare final accounts from the year ended 31-3-2014.**

Name of Account	L.F	Debit Balance	Credit Balance
Capital and drawings		750	25,000
Sales		-	3,70,000
Purchase		3,49,600	-
Salary		600	-
Carriage inward		200	-
Carriage outward		250	-
Factory exp		150	-
Rates, taxes and insurance		200	-
Discount		-	250
Vehicles		15,000	-
Furniture		3000	-
Creditors		-	10,000
Debtors		4000	-
Cash and bank balance		875	-
Stock (Dt : 31-3-2014)		30,625	-
		4,05,250	4,05,250

Adjustments

(1) Material purchased of vehicles of **Rs.500** is wrongly debited to purchase account.

(2) **Rs. 250** of furniture is wrongly debited to drawings account.

(3) **Rs. 250** received from Shalini debtor is wrongly credited sales account.

(4) Calculate deprecation on vehicles at **5%** and furniture at **8 %**.

(5) Write off **Rs. 50** from debtors as bad debt and provide **5 %** bad debt reserve. Insurance prepaid is of **Rs. 75** and carriage outward of **Rs. 150** is yet to be paid.

3. From the following trial balance of Ket prepare final accounts for the year ended 31-3-2015.

Debit-Balance	Amount Rs.	Credit- Balance	Amount Rs.
Trading account (cr)	38,580	Bills receivable	12,810
Capital	75,000	Bills payable	4200
Drawings	22,500	Closing stock	19,170
Building	24,000	Discount (cr)	900
Office expenses	960	Bad debts	600
Bank overdraft	3600	Prepaid insurance	4749
Rent	2250	Creditors	18,000
Rates, taxes and insurance	6000	Travelling exp	2400
Salary	6000	Carriage outward	1740
Machinery	30,000	Bad debts reserve	1950
Sundry debtors	13,500	o/s stationery expenses	4449

Adjustments:

1) calculate interest on capital at **5%.**

2) deprecation on machinery and building at 5%

3) interest on bank overdraft **Rs. 225** is yet to be paid.

4) write off **Rs. 900** as bad debt from debtors provide **5%** bad debts reserve.

5) after preparing trading account it was found that ket has taken goods for personal use of **Rs. 1500** which is not recorded in books

.

4. The following is the trial balance of Chailtali as on 31-3-2012

Name of Account	L.F	Debit	Credit
Capital and drawings		3500	56,000
Debts and receivable		13,710	12,100
Purchases and sales		61,000	77,000
Good returns		700	1400
Stock (opening)		3500	-
Carriage inward		350	-
Salary		5,720	-
Wages		760	-
Advertisement expenses		910	-
Taxes		280	-
Postage and stationery exp		1050	-
Insurance premium		420	-
Commission		-	210
Rent		-	480
Dividend		-	200
Goods given for advertisement		-	920
Bad debts		280	-
Building		35,000	-
Furniture		2800	-
Investment in shares		4000	-
Leasehold building		14,000	-
Cash balance		330	-
		1,48,310	1,48,310

Adjustments :

1) The cost price of closing stock is **Rs. 12,300** but its market value is **Rs. 9600.**

2) The salary is for **11** months. Salary for march **2012** is outstanding.

3) **Rs. 300** being insurance premium for the year ending on **30-9-2012** is included in the insurance premium

4) Commission of **Rs. 150** is receivable, whereas rent is received for the **12** months ending as on **31-5-2012**.

5) Write off **Rs. 310** from debtors and provide **5%** bad debts reserve on debtors.

6) The period of lease on building is **10** years. furniture was purchased on **1-10-2011**

7) Capital of **Rs. 16,000** is brought on **30-9-2011,** and drawings are made on **1-12-2011** calculate

   10 % interest on capital and **12%** interest on drawings p.a.

5.   Zeel operates a provision stores. The ratio of his capital and general reserve is **3 : 1** in the business. The balances of other accounts on that date are as under. Prepare final accounts.

Debit-Balance	Rs.	Credit-Balance	Rs.
Opening stock	21,000	Advertisement	4000
Purchases	32,000	Provision for bad debts	500
Sales	50,000	Rent(**Rs. 150 p.m**)	1650
Debtors	16,000	Patents	14000
Machinery	60,000	Carriage inward	2150
10 % loan taken from	5,000	Creditors	18000
Pankaj from (**1-10-2003**)		Cash balance	3000
Insurance premium	2,500	Office salary	3200
furniture	16,000	Rent received	2000

Adjustments:

1) Closing stock is **Rs. 1,00,000** of which market value of **10%** goods is **20 %** less.

2) Goods of **Rs. 2000** are distributed free as samples, which are yet to be recorded.

3) Goods of **Rs. 4000** withdrawn by Zeel for his personal use are recorded in the sales book. Purchase invoice of **Rs.** 1000 is not recorded in the purchase book.

4) Calculate **10 %** interest on capital.

5) **Rs. 1600** paid for the year ending as **30-6-2004** is included in insurance premium.

6) A debtor of **Rs. 8000** out of total debtors is declared insolvent and his receiver has declared first and final dividend of **75** paise per rupee. Provide **5%** bad debts reserve on debtors.

7) Calculate **10 %** depreciation on machinery. Patents to be revaluated at **Rs. 12,800**

8) Office salary of **Rs. 1200** is outstanding.

6. From the following trial balance and adjustment of Chintan as on **31-3-2009**. Prepare final account.

Name of Account	L. F	Debit Balance	Credit Balance
Capital and drawings		40,000	1,50,000
Customers and suppliers		30,000	10,000
Provident fund and its contributions		1000	6000
Investments of provident fund and its interest		5000	500
Cash and bank		2000	15,000
Salary 11 months upto (29-2-09)		16500	-
Advertisements exp		2000	-
Postage exp		3000	-
Leasehold building (for 10 years 1-10-2008)		500	-
Machinery		100000	-
Insurance premium		40000	-
Commission		4000	6000
Bills		-	7600
Stock of Goods		11000	-
Advertisements Suspense a/c		19000	-
Bad debts and bed reserve		30000	3600
Trading A/c		1600	1,06,900
		3,05,600	3,05,600

Adjustments:

(1) Stationery stock is **Rs. 200** as **31-3-2009.**

(2) Advertisement expense incurred at the beginning of the year is recorded as advertisement suspense a/c and it is to be written off over 5 years

(3) Wages of **Rs. 2000** are outstanding.

(4) Goods withdrawn for personal use of **Rs. 1000** on **31-3-2009** are yet to be recorded.

(5) Write off bad debts of **Rs. 1000** from debtors and **Rs. 1800** is to be reduced from the bad debts reserve.

(6) Machinery of **Rs. 20,000** is purchased on **1-10-08.** Calculate deprecation of **10 %&** p.a on machinery.

(7) Credit sales of **Rs. 7000** is yet to be recorded.

7. Prepare final accounts from the following trial balance and adjustments of Hemang :

Debit-Balance	Amount	Credit- Balance	Amount
Opening stock	8,000	Capital	1,80,000
Purchases	64,000	Sales	1,93,000
drawings	10,000	Purchase-returns	2000
Sales return	3000	Discount-received	1600
Freight and octroi	4000	Provision for bad debts	1800
Sales tax	10,200	Bad debts return	1080
Salary (upto 29-2-2004)	19,800	Interest on 14% debentures	1120
Insurance premium (For the year ending on 31-12-2004)	4800	Bank loan creditors	16,000
Carriage outward	16,400	creditors	12,000
Discount allowed	1120	Suspense a/c	12,000
Bad debts	400		
Investments in 14% debentures (from 1-4-2003)	16,000		
Building	1,90,000		
Patents	16,400		
Debtors	37,200		
Cash	14,480		
Building repairing a/c	4800		
	4,20,600		4,20,600

<u>*Adjustments :*</u>

1) *Closing stock is of* **Rs. 28,000**
2) *Write off* **Rs. 1200** *from debtors and provide* **5%** *bad debts reserve, also provide included in building on debtors.*
3) **Rs. 1600** *of personal repairing are included in building repairing*
4) **20%** *amount of sales is export sales, on which* **5%** *subsidy is yet to be received.*
5) *The value of patents is to be treated at* **Rs. 14,400**
6) *Calculate* **5%** *depreciation on tax refund of* **Rs. 1000** *is yet to received.*

8. *From the following Trial Balance as on* **31-3-2014** *and adjustments of Kesha prepare final accounts.*

Name of Account	L.F	Debit	Credit
Capital			70,000
Drawings		4000	-
Stock (1-4-2013)		16,000	-
Purchases		1,06,000	-
Sales			1,08,000
Goods Returns		3,200	4000
Salary		8800	-
Audit Fees		400	-
Rates and taxes		1000	-
Stationery-printing		2000	-
Outstanding Salary		-	800
Prepaid insurance premium		400	-
Insurance premium		2000	-
Wages		3060	-
Freight and octroi		500	-
Demurrage and dock charges		440	-
Carriage In ward		800	-
Carriage outward		960	-
Commission		-	1600
Rent		-	4000
Bed Debt		1200	-
Debtors		4000	-
Creditors		-	20,880
Building		32000	-
Additional Building (Dt : 31-12-13)		8000	-
Cash and bank balance		7920	-
Vehicle		8000	-
Bills		2400	2000
		2,11,280	2,11,280

Adjustments :

1) Closing Stock is of **Rs. 16000** But market value of **Rs. 4000** stock is less by **10 %.**

2) Bed debts reserve at **5%** on debtors and discount reserve at **2 %** is required.

3) Rent of **Rs. 800** is yet to be received and commission of **Rs. 200** is received in advance.

4) Provide deprecations on building at **5%**

5) The estimated life of vehicle is approx. **5** years and at the expiry of the same period the scrap value is estimated at **Rs. 1000.**

6) calculated interest on capital at **6 %** on **30-11-2013** additional capital of **Rs. 10,000** was brought into the business, interest on drawings **Rs. 150** is to be charged.

7) Provision of **Rs. 200** is made on bills receivable.

8) The purchase invoice of **Rs. 2000** was not recorded. But the same was included in stock.

9. From the trial balance of **31-12-10** and other information prepare final accounts .

Debit Balances	*Amount Rs.*	*Credit Balances*	*Amount Rs.*
Drawings	24,000	Capital	71,400
Purchases	1,04,000	Sales	1,84,000
Goods return	1,600	Goods return	1,200
Stock of goods (1-01-10)	16,000	Provision for bad debts	2,000

Salaries	18,000	Bank loan	13,500
Office expenses	9,000	Traders	40,000
Carriage inward	3,000	Bills Payable	1,800
Carriage outward	4,500	General reserve	8,000
Bad debts	1,400	Loan acquired	4,000
Customers	67,000	Brokerage	1,600
Bills receivable	2,000		
Cash and Bank	5,600		
Investments	14,000		
Machines	24,000		
Lease-hold building (From **1-01-10** for **5** years)	30,000		
Insurance premium (Including **Rs. 2,400** for the year ending on **31-03-11**)	3,400		
	3,27,500		3,27,500

Adjustments :

1. Closing stock was **Rs. 28,600** ,out of which the market value of **10%** goods is **20%** less.

2. Investments are valued at **Rs. 12,000.**

3. ¾ Brokerage is received in advance.

4. Unpaid salary **Rs. 2,000.**

5. Write off **Rs. 1,000** as bad debts from debtors and make a provision for bad debts reserve at **5%**

........xxxxxxxxx......

CHAPTER – 5
("Accounting concepts, principles and conventions")

🗋 THEORY SECTION 🗋

❖ Accounting concepts, principles and conventions

Lets us study the accounting concepts and principles which form a part of the syllabi for standard 11, out of all those principles which are followed in recording business transactions, and preparing financial statements.

(1) Basic assumptions of accounting :-
   - ✓ Accounting entry or separate entry
   - ✓ Money measurement
   - ✓ Going concern
   - ✓ Accounting period

(1) Accounting entry : according to this, it is assumed that business has the separate existence and its entity is different from that of its owner.

(2) According is done for only those transactions and events which affect that business. Personal transactions of owner which are not affecting business are not recorded in the books of accounts of business when the owner of a business bring capital into business, it is credited to owner's capital account. Such capital is known as liability of business to its owner.

Capital + liabilities = Total assets

$C + L = A$

This equation also suggests that the owner is an entity different from the business.

Money Measurement : *in business, all transactions are represented in monetary unit, for accounting money is accepted as common measurement unit. Economic worth of assets and liabilities are stated in monetary terms instead of their physical quantity. The transactions, which cannot be measured in terms of money are not recorded in accounts, though physical units are involved in financial transactions accounting thereof is made in terms of common measurement unit of money only. This concept has two important limitations*

(1) The transactions and events affecting business, though important, are not recorded in the books of accounts of business if they cannot be measured in terms of money.

(3) *The second limitation emerges from the principle of stable value of money. According to this concept, value of money remains stable every year or the changes in the value of money is immaterial and hence of no significance. Therefore, the value of money does not change for a long time. In spite of this, the accounts prepared based on the historical cost at the time when the transaction has taken place have proved to be useful to various users of financial statements.*

(4) Going Concern : *according to this concept, it is assumed that the business concern will continue for a long period and the same will not be closed or liquidated in the near future.*

business associates like creditors, lenders, etc. also deal business concern or enter into long term contracts with the business concern with an assumption that the business will continue for a long period. According depreciated values and market values of fixed assets are not taken into account. Fixed assets will be used for a long time in future and they are not purchased for resale.

Prepaid expenses are also shown on the asset of balance sheet because of the assumption that the business will continue for a long time and it is expected that the firm shall get the benefit of such prepaid expenses in future deferred revenue expenditures are also shown on the asset side to balance sheet based on this concept. Going concern concept is sometimes proved to be less utility, as in the following events or circumstances.

(a)When the object for which a business was established is achieved or is likely to be accomplished in near future

(b) when an industrial unit is declared sick.

(c) when a business is passing through severe financial crises and is likely to be liquidated very shortly.

(d) when a liquidator is appointed for liquidation of a company.

Accounting period :

Accounting period is related to going concern concept. The going concern concept implies that the business activities will continue indefinitely. If this assumption is accepted, complete picture of profit or loss can be known only at the time of liquidation of the business, but it is not possible for a businessman to wait till the closure of business. Therefore, the life of business is divided into specific accounting period, this is known as accounting period, at the end of each such accounting period, financial statements are prepared. Such accounting period is of 12 months. According results are also prepared at the end of every year because the period of 12 months covers the effects of various seasons on the business therefore the accounts are also known as annual accounts. Such an accounting year could be a calendar year, a samvat year, a financial year a co-operative year or any other period in India, according to income tax law firms are required to furnish the details of income for income tax based on accounts prepared for a financial year.

Basic Principles :

(1) Duality :

Duality or dual aspect is a basic and a very important principle of accounting. According to this principle every business transaction has a twofold effect (i) from the angle of benefit received (ii) From the angle of benefit given.

" *every receiver is a giver and every giver is a receiver* "*for recording this twofold effect in the books of accounts, accounting terminology of ' debit' and ' credit' are used. The structure of according is a based on this concept of duality and accounting equation or balance sheet equation is also based on this principle of duality. Thus, total debit effects and total credit effects of various transactions posted in the ledger accounts are always equal.*

(2) Verifiability and objectivity of evidence :

accounting information should be free from personal opinion and basis. Accounting information should be verifiable by any outsiders for verifiability of accounting information documentary evidences are necessary thus, with the help of vouchers, accounts can be prepared which are free from the personal basis of the owner, manager, or accountant. Such accounts can be considered reliable.

For some transactions, vouchers are not available such transactions could also be important from the view point of business. For example, no voucher is available for provision or depreciation or bad debts reserve. Under such circumstances, note on policy decision of management could be accepted as an evidence and accordingly vouchers are prepared.

(3) Revenue Recognition (according to Historical cost) : *according to this principle, revenue is recognized as income of the period in which the same is earned or received. In case of sale of goods, the revenue is considered as recognized when the ownership in the goods is transferred.*

Professionals like doctors, advocates, chartered accountants etc. cannot file a suit against their patients or clients due to professional code of conduct. They recognize revenue only when the amount of fee is received in cash. Thus, they maintain accounts on mercantile basis. According to mercantile system, fees will be recognized as revenue as soon as the same becomes receivable.

While preparing the accounts of gold mines, an entry is passed at selling price as soon as gold is produced from mines and not when the actual sale is made.

(4) Matching cost with revenue concept :
For determining the are compared with total revenue expenses and the difference profit or loss of a given period, total revenue of the given accounting period is comp aired with total expenses for that period. if the income or revenue is more than the expenses, the difference between the two is known as profit. If the expenses are more than the revenue or income, the difference is known as loss. Thus, for determining the profit or loss of an accounting period, total

revenue incomes is ascertained . this is known as the concept of matching cost with revenue.

In business, some expenses are associated with time. Some expenses are not associated with a definite time period or a particular income. Deprecation on fixed assets is also worked out based on a particular method and is appropriated against the income of a respective period.

(5) Full disclosure :

According to this principle, all material information should be disclosed in the financial statements. To enable the users of the financial statements to take correct economic decisions, it is necessary to disclose all the relevant information in the financial statements no material information affecting the interests of general investors should remain undisclosed or concealed financial statements should be prepared honestly.

♣ Modifying principles :

(1)   Materiality :

This concept is associated with the principle of full disclosure. According to full disclosure principle, all material information should be disclosed in financial statements. Materiality depends upon relevance and reliability of information, thus information would be considered as material only when the same is relevant and significant.

According to this concept, any information would be shown in detail in financial statements only when the same is useful to the users of such information. Thus accountant is not required to disclose in account or in financial statements any immaterial transactions.

Materiality also depends on the amount involved in a transaction.

It is not possible to give a definite rule for determining the materiality in each case. It depends upon the quantum of amount, relevance and importance of such an item or a transaction in the business.

(2) **Consistency :**

The principle of consistency suggests that while writing accounts or preparing financial statements, the same policies, procedures and methods should be followed every year. Comparison of accounts and trend analysis can be possible only if the principle of consistency is followed. Sometimes consistency is not maintained with an objective of accounting frauds. If consistency is not maintained in accounting, the accounts may not remain dependable and can also mislead at times.

(3) **Prudence :**

An accountant does not take into account anticipated gain or profit to be received in future but provides for all anticipated losses.

For example closing stock is valued at cost or market price whichever is less. If cost of closing stock at the end of the year is **Rs. 50,000** *and its market price is* **Rs. 40,000.** *Closing stock shall be shown at* **Rs. 40,000** *on credit side of trading account. As a result, effect of anticipated loss of* **Rs. 10,000** *will be there in trading account. At the same time, if market value of this closing stock is* **Rs. 60,000** *its cost* **Rs.50,000** *only will be taken on the credit side of trading account. Thus, anticipated profit of* **Rs. 10,000** *is not taken into account As the same is not actually realized. This is how the tendency of businessman is reflected in accounts. This approach is also known as concept of " Conservatism"*

Similarly, in the accounts, provisions for doubtful debts, discount reserve on debtors, contingent liabilities, repairs and fluctuation in value of investments are made based on the principle of prudence only.

According to this principle, all research and development expenses are debited to the profit and loss account of the year in which they are incurred even if the benefit of such expenses is derived in future.

This concept suffers from the limitation of creating secret reserve, which in neither fair nor legal, if assets are understated by making higher provisions and profit are understated by providing for more expenses.

At present, the principles of consistency, full disclosure, materiality and objectivity are given more importance. This principle is applied only if there is no conflict with other principles.

(4) Timeliness :

According to this principle, the user of accounting information should get the required information and at the time when required. Generally, accounting information is given in the form of annual reports at the end of the accounting year. Such an information cannot become useful to management for control purpose. Similarly investors should also get information at regular intervals to enable them to make their investment decisions. Therefore, many companies prepare and publish interim accounts which are very useful to management and investors.

Such interim information can help in decision making if the same is provided on monthly, quarterly, or half yearly basis.

(5) Substance over form :

It is essential to comply with the respective legal provisions while preparing accounts. When accounts are to be presented in a form prescribed by law, the appropriate accounting information has to be furnished in the form matching with such a requirement of law. However, in such cases, meaningful presentation should be given more importance than the more than form. Instead of keeping only legal form into mind. The accounts should be presented in accordance with the substance and financial reality.

(6) Variations in accounting practices :

There are variations in accounting practices for certain matters and hence it may happen that the same event can be presented differently in financial statements some such instances of diverse practices are discussed below.

(i) *should fixed assets be disclosed in balance sheet at historical cost or at revalued amount at current purchasing power value or at current cost price ?*

(ii) *by which method should deprecation be calculated on fixed assets ? by fixed installment method by reducing balance method or by any other method ? depreciation calculated according to each of the methods will show different amounts of depreciation and hence different amounts of fixed assets in the balance sheet.*

(iii) *Which method of stock valuation should be adopted ? By FIFO (First in First Out) method or by LIFO (Last in First Out) method or by weighted average method ? any method adopted out of these methods will given difference amount for cost of goods sold and closing stock.*

(iv) *Should research and development expenses be considered as capital, revenue or differed revenue expenditure ?*

(v) *How much amount should be provided as reserve for doubtful debts?*

(vi) *How should investments be valued?*

(vii) *How much provision should be made for accidental or confinement liabilities?*

(viii) *What should be the treatment of profit or loss arising out of conversion of foreign currency transactions into rupees?*

(ix) *How to record transactions and installments and calculate profits in respect of hire purchase transactions lease transactions and installment transactions ?*

(x) *How much profit or loss should be recognized every year in respect of long term contracts?*

(xi) *What should be the accounting arrangement for goodwill, patents and trademarks?*

(xii) *Accounting for profit or loss on sale of fixed assets made by different methods.*

Accounting standard :

Meaning of accounting standard :

Accounting standards are the set of rules to present financial statements in the form of a report and they are issued by professional accounting bodies at regular intervals. the *objective of accounting standards is to harmonies diverse accounting of practices and policies used in preparing accounts. This accounting standards are applicable all the enterprises or to a particular practice of such enterprises.*

History of accounting standards :

we shall just get information on history of accounting standers this information about history is not for examination history of accounting standards can be divided into three stages.

1) *First stage period is during **1932** to **1940** when an attempt was made to study accounting knowledge. Which came to be known as accounting principles.*

2) *Second stage is during **1938** to **1973** during which accounting professions gave rules which were provided logical support by the professional working in the field of accountancy.*

3) *Third stage is from **1973** till today wherein attempts are made at national and international level to frame various accounting standards the efforts to formulate accounting standards on more and more accounting aspects are continuing even today.*

> *International accounting standards committee (IASC) was established in 1973 in which 9 countries namely, Australia, France, Germany Japan Mexico, Netherlands Britain and Ireland and U.S.A were founder members. Thereafter professional accounting*

bodies of many more countries joined IASC. Institute of chartered accountants of India also became member of IASC. This board has issued 41 accounting standards so far and they are accepted in India as well.

Form of accounting standard :

(i) *First part deals subject matter of the standard and the mode of implementation of the standard*

(ii) *The second part contains introduction which deals with the need for the standard on the subject matter, what are the current practices of accounting in respect of the subject of the standard discusses the diversities and limitation ions of the current practices.*

(iii) *Third part gives definitions of the terms used in the standard and explains background of the standard with detailed explanation on details contained in main part of the standard with detailed explanation on details contained in main part of the recommended standards.*

(iv) *The fourth part contains main text of the standard and recommendation to follow the same.*

Need for accounting standard :

1) Uniformaslity is brought in preparing accounts and financial statements

2) Accounting standards are useful for comparison of

accounting standard.

3) Accounts become objective and reliable by following accounting standards.

4) Because of accounting standards, comparison of different years as also of different firms becomes possible.

5) Accounting standards provide useful information to government in framing law relating to accounting matters.

6) Accounting standards also become useful to auditors, if the accounts are not maintained following accounting standards, auditors can resort to detailed scrutiny and can unearth accounting frauds.

7) Accounting standards are also useful to the accountant in his accounting work. If he follows accounting standards personal opinions or bias does not creep in accounts.

………xxxxxxxx……

CHAPTER – 6
("Rectification of Errors")

☐ THEORY SECTION ☐

Irrespective of whether the accounting errors are committed innocently or intentionally they cannot be rectified by erasing with the help of an eraser. Necessary accounting effects are to be given in accounts in order to rectify these errors. Sometimes if an error affects two accounts, in order to rectify the same, a journal entry is passed which is known as a rectification entry and it is recorded in journal proper.

Generally two principles should be taken into consideration to rectify the accounting errors.

➤ **Undo what is wrong.**
   Do what is correct.

❖ *Types of Accounting Errors :-*

   ➤ *Errors which do not affect the trial balance.*
   ➤ *Errors which affect the trial balance.*

❖ ***Errors not Affecting the Trial Balance***

1) Errors of Omission : *When a transaction is totally omitted to be recorded in the journal or the subsidiary book or the ledger such an error is known as an error of omission.*

By writing correct journal entry for this transaction the above error will be rectified.

2) Errors of Principal :

When an error arises because of non- compliance of accounting principles it is known as an error of principle. Because of ignorance of principles of accountancy, when instead of one account, any other account is debited or credited, error of principle occurs.

3) Errors of Recording to a Wrong Account :

In such type of an error, journal entry is written correctly but while posting, instead of giving the effect to the correct account by mistake the effect is given to some other account. Thus by debiting or crediting a wrong account with correct amount, on the correct side, the trial balance remains unaffected.

4) Errors Committed at the time of Recording in primary Books:(Errors of commission)
While writing the books of accounts, due to

negligence if the transaction in primary books are recorded with more or less than the correct amount or are recorded in wrong subsidiary books such an error is known as an error of Commission.

- ✓ Transaction Recorded in Correct Book with less Amount
- ✓ Transaction Recorded in Correct book With more Amount : In this Case original will be reversed with the amount of difference.
- ✓ Transaction recorded in Wrong Subsidiary Book : In this type of error, instead of recording the transaction in the correct subsidiary book, it is recorded in another subsidiary book.
- ✓ Transaction Recorded in wrong subsidiary book with wrong Amount.
- ✓

5) Compensatory Errors :

In the book of accounts when more than one error exists but because of their nullifying effect on both debit and credit side the trial balance tallies, such errors are known as compensatory errors.

❖ Errors Affecting the Trial Balance :

1) Errors Regarding Posting :

☆ ***Omission of Posting :*** *While posting the transaction recorded in journal or subsidiary books, of posting is omitted in any account by mistake, it is known as an error of omission of posting and in this case the trial balance does not tally.*

☆ ***Posting Twice in an Account :***
Out of the two accounts affected, if in any one account posting is done on the correct side but twice by an error, the trial balance will not tally.

☆ ***Posting of a Wrong Amount in an Account :***
While posting from the primary books if a wrong amount is posted in any account, the trial balance does not tally.

☆ ***Posting in an Account on the Wrong Side :***
While posting from the primary books, if the amount is posted on the wrong side the trial balance does not tally (On credit side instead of debit or vice versa)

☆ ***Posting Wrong Amount on the Wrong Side of an Account :***
In this case, posting is done in an account on the wrong side and that too of a wrong amount.

2) Errors Regarding Balance of an Account :

✗ Error in Finding out the Balance of an Account :

If the balance of any account is found more or less the trial balance does not tally. If the calculated balance is less, Put the deficit amount on the correct side to rectify the error.

✗ Error in Writing the balance of an Account :

In this case the balance is calculated correctly but when it is brought forward it is written a wrong amount and therefore the trial balance does not tally.

✗ Balance of an account is Omitted to be Recorded :

If the opening balance of any account remains unrecorded, the trial balance does not tally.

✗ Balance of an Account is written on the Wrong Side

By mistake if the balance of any account is written on the opposite side (Written on credit side instead of debit side and viceversa)the tally balance does not tally.

✗ Balance Of an account is written on the wrong side with a wrong :

The trial balance does not tally if the balance of any account is written on the wrong side with a wrong amount.

3) Errors in Totaling the subsidiary Books :

The trial balance does not tally if an error is committed while totaling subsidiary books like purchase book, sales book. Goods return book, cash book, etc This error will be rectified by writing necessary note in that respective account. A journal entry is not necessary to rectify this type of error.

4) Errors committed while preparing Trial Balance :

While preparing the trial balance there remains a possibility of errors like, Error in totaling of the trial balance, balance of an account is omitted to be recorded, is recorded twice is recorded with wrong amount, is recorded on the wrong side, or is recorded on wrong side with the wrong amount.

In order to rectify these types of errors no journal entry is required. After rectifying the errors, a new trial balance is prepared and it will get tallied.

❖ **Suspense account and errors detected after preparation of the final Accounts :**

If the accounts are written accurately without any error, the trial balance tallies and thereafter final accounts are prepared. But when trial balance does not tally. Because of same errors, too much time is required to detect such errors and consequently final accounts can not be prepared in time. In such circumstances the difference of the trial balance is transferred to a suspense account and final accounts are prepared. Afterwards the suspense account is closed, When after detection errors are rectified with or without the help of suspense account as per requirements. Suspense account will be closed automatically when all errors rectified.

⇒ **Suspense Account :**

When the trial balance does not tally because of some accounting errors and it requires more time to prepare final account after detection and rectification of such errors, but there is an urgency for preparing final accounts, temporarily the difference in the trial balance is transferred to one account, in order to get it tallied and that account is known as a Suspense Account.

If the difference arises on the debit side of trial balance it is treated as a debit balance of suspense account and in final accounts it will be shown on the assets side of the balance sheet.

If the difference arises on the credit side of a trial balance, it is treated as credit balance of suspense account and in final accounts it will be shown on the Capital-Liabilities side of the balance sheet.

⇒ **Uses of Suspense Account :**

Other than rectification of errors, suspense account is useful for various other account is to be credited to suspense account is useful for various other purpose such as,

1. *When in any transaction which account is to be debited or credited not decide, for the time being that amount is debited or credited to suspense account. Later on when the correct head of account is decide, after effect to that account, Suspense account is closed.*

2. *When in any transaction, if the name of the party is to be kept secret, that amount is recorded to suspense account.*

❖ **Effects of Rectification on Profit-Loss :**

For preparing final accounts an error affecting asset or personal accounts, do not affect the

P & L of the business but an error affecting the accounts of goods (such as purchase A/c, Sales A/c, goods Return A/c outflow of goods by other way a/c etc.) Affects P & L a/c of business, in rectification, if accounts regarding goods or income – expenses are debited, profit will be decreased or loss will be increased in rectification, if accounts regarding goods or income- expenses are credited, Profit will be increased or loss will be decreased.

☐ PRACTICAL SECTION ☐

1. **At the time of preparing final accounts of Sandeep as on 31-12-2013. The following errors are found out. Pass necessary rectification entries to rectify the same:**

1) **Rs. 2000** paid for purchased of a typewriter is debited to purchase account at the time of posting from cash book.

2) **Rs. 2400** paid for rent to Dharmnandan a owner of shop, by mistake is debited to his personal account.

3) Goods of **Rs. 4500** are completely burnt by fire and insurance Co. has accepted a claim at **40%** for the same, no entry has been pass in books.

4) **Rs. 600** paid for brokerage is posted twice in brokerage A/c

5) **Rs. 30,000** incurred for extension of building, by mistake is debited to repairing expense account.

6) **Rs. 21** paid for general expense is posted to that account as **Rs. 221.**

7) **Rs. 430** received towards interest, is posted to interest account on debit side.

8) A machinery of **Rs. 9600** is sold for **Rs. 10,500** it is recorded in sales book at **Rs. 10,500.**

9) Total of bills payable book is under cast by **Rs. 870.**

10)   In December **2003** discount received and discount paid are **Rs. 530** and **Rs. 680** respectively. But by mistake, they are recorded on their opposite sides.

2. **Trial balance of Neeta for the year 2014 does not tally and therefore a difference of Rs. 2460 is credited to suspense account. The following errors are detected after final accounts are prepared.**

   1) Total of sales return book is under cast by **Rs. 270.**

   2) **Rs. 450** received from Kapilaben was written off as bad debts in past years. This amount is credited to her personal account.

   3) A Cheque of **Rs. 2910** is received from Jyotsanaben, is posted in her account on debit side by **Rs. 2370.**

   4) Life insurance premium of **Rs. 3600** is debited to insurance premium account.

   5) Purchase of machine of **Rs. 7500** is recorded in purchase book.

6) Advance salary of **Rs. 3000** paid to Ritaben is debited to salary account.

7) Opening balance of **Rs. 750** of Hansaben a debtor's account id written in her account on credit side.

8) Cash sales of **Rs. 1770** is posted in sales account as **Rs. 2850.**

9) **Rs. 1110** received from Meghaben is credited in her account as **Rs. 1080**

10) Bank charges of **Rs. 45** are left unrecorded.

3. **Trial balance of Sushma for the year ending 2015 does not tally and there for final accounts are prepared by transferring the difference to a suspense account. Thereafter following errors are found out, to rectify these errors pass necessary rectification entries, prepare suspense a/c, and show the effects of rectification on profit-loss.**

1) A cash payment of **Rs. 1750** for the purchase of a typewriter, is debited to office expenses A/c.

2) Goods of **Rs. 2000** sold to Satyendra are correctly, recorded in sales book but are posted as **Rs. 2500** in Satyendra's A/c.

3) Total of sales book for the month of December is overcast by **Rs. 500.**

4) Goods of **Rs. 650** returned by Jayesh are recorded in sales book and are credited to Jayesh's a/c.

5) Goods of **Rs. 350** sold to Pravin for cash, are correctly recorded in cash book but in sales ledger, the same are credited to Pravin's Account.

6) A bill receivable of **Rs. 8000** received from Prafulchandra is credited to bills payable account and to Prafulchandra's account too.

7) Sales return book total is overcast by **Rs. 50**.

8) A balance of furniture account is carried forward as **Rs. 800** instead of **Rs. 750**.

4. *A bookkeeper found his Trial Balance not balanced, placed The difference amount in the Suspense Account and subsequently found the following errors:*

a) Sales Book was overcast by **Rs.** 2,500.

b) **Rs.** 2000 received from Vani in full settlement of his account of **Rs.** 1,000 was posted in cash book but omitted to be entered in her account.

c) The total of the sales book **Rs.** 2,000 was debited to sales returns account.

d) **Rs.** 2,000 received as interest was credited to interest account as **Rs.** 100.

Give rectifying entries and show the Suspense Account.

5. *An Accountant could not tally the trial balance. The difference of Rs. 520 was temporarily placed to the credit of suspense Account and subsequently found the following errors.*

a) The total of the discount column on the credit side of the cash Book **Rs.** 230 was not posted in the ledger.

b) The total of the discount column on the debit side of the cash Book **Rs.** 150 was omitted to be posted in the ledger.

c) The total of the purchases book was short by **Rs.** 600.

d) A sale of **Rs.**675 to Kalpana was entered in the Sales book as **Rs.** 975.

e) A sale of **Rs.**500 to Vimala has been entered in the Purchase Book.Rectify the above errors through Suspense Account. Also give journal entries for rectification.

………xxxxxxxxx……

www.ingramcontent.com/pod-product-compliance
Lightning Source LLC
Chambersburg PA
CBHW080836180526
45168CB00006B/2706